All the Names Between

All the Names Between

Julia McCarthy

Brick Books

Library and Archives Canada Cataloguing in Publication

McCarthy, Julia, 1964–, author
All the names between / Julia McCarthy.

Poems.
Issued also in electronic formats.
ISBN 978-1-77131-457-2 (softcover).—ISBN 978-1-77131-459-6
(PDF).—ISBN 978-1-77131-458-9 (EPUB)

I. Title.

PS8575.C4186A79 2017 C811'.6 C2016-907491-9
C2016-907492-7

We acknowledge the Canada Council for the Arts, the Government of Canada
through the Canada Book Fund, and the Ontario Arts Council for their support of
our publishing program.

The author photo was taken by Mary Anne McCarthy.
The book is set in Dante.
The cover painting is by Wayne Boucher: "Between April and May"
(oil on canvas, 36" x 36", 2014).
Design and layout by Marijke Friesen.
Printed and bound by Sunville Printco Inc.

Brick Books
431 Boler Road, Box 20081
London, Ontario N6K 4G6

www.brickbooks.ca

Not of flesh and blood, but
of the stars in the flesh
and blood . . .
—Paracelsus

I have a hankering for the dust-light, for all things illegible.
—Charles Wright

CONTENTS

○

Proem

There you are my little seed
my little blackness   splitting
sprouting filament   breathflicker
shoot tasting the air
death's husks at your side
wooden twins   Trojan bowls
burning   burning
the shine of your fallen light.

A Stab in the Dark

Tonight the crescent moon is on its back
facing the darkness and I know that feeling
of nightfulness and the half ring it leaves
like part of a cupmark on a walnut table
so I listen to coyotes threading the forest
the warp and weft of being and nonbeing
steeking the gap   choiring all that isn't
the unsung fraying like the slip
of a moon on its back   horns like incisors
a stab in the dark   bitemark of stars
as the forest tightens for the night.

Seance

I come to sit
and silently call out to the energies
threaded through the eyes of words

I call out to the dead
who are the most energetic of all
the trace of their red hands still waving
from cave walls

I listen to the long strings
light years
of history and prehistory
preverbal as the original ditch
of nothingness
and matter's first gasp
the bang   tap and slide
across Ouija space
all the negative music   echoes
and whispers of nebulas
wrapping their rust and green scarves
around particles of dust
blindfolding the words.

Woundless

The poplars have sent all their letters
I study them like palms
this one tells me what's to come
how good and green the place
it last saw was
this one indicates what is woundless
that I must learn to walk among the dead
with perfect calm

a crow slicks back the sky
autumn's incisors sink in
everything a bit wounded   bits of flesh
masquerading as clouds
a little something missing in the husking earth
leaves raked and burned like letters
smoke in the clothes of things
a few sparks fading
as the doe in the orchard fades
without moving
a watercolour unpainting itself
the season's rough tongue
dissolving the bandages.

Disjecta Membra

I'm folded into my chair
exhausted
everywhere I look
two splashes of light
and a bouquet of flies
the dead have thrown away

it's a paradoxical wedding

in this place words collapse
like tents
their sighs dissolving
like another skin
in the pitched world

flesh of my flesh
the slow locust tree
tests the air
wading into its green tragedy

in the shade
finches swing their gold
hammocks between invisible poles
the way metaphors swing over the abyss

beware of heights and rickety words
admire those who need no such bridges

yin gulls circling
poplars in their green offices
shuffling their papers
pebbles parked in soil
like studs against earlobes

the earth is earthing

mid-June
winter in drag
in the field mallows
the colour of gossip
put their heads together like young girls
goldenrod slow dances
in the sun
a strand of children is cut
from an orange bus
they roll across the street
bright as beads

at my feet
a wounded beetle pulls
the earth like a rope
unable to free itself
completely from the wreck
from the cause and effect
with really sharp teeth

this is what dying is like

your mind outgrows
your body like a river
flooding the city

buildings like vertebrae
bone of your bone
white antennae
sensing the insensible

so that the grass bends
beneath the weight of this bloodless blood
so that you no longer mistake
all its sorrows for a breeze

so that a sparrow pulls its suitcase
of feathers into green windows
closed against the heat
and opens
spilling its jewellery
beads like children
feathers like petals
from an impossible flower
the way locust petals detach
floating white as cells
disjecta membra
the slow dissolve
burn-off of fog like words
from the bloom

the river rises
the sound of drowning grass
is a feather turning like a key
an ash key turning water
an ostiary opening door after door so fluid

they're hardly there
while your hair trails its green path
like a bridge made of grass.

An Ocean Field

It's no wonder I've always wanted a view of the sea
having come from there in the first and second place
I understand the fluid nature of that liquid land
in this body composed mostly of water
on this spinning sphere likewise made
I have a house facing a forest sea and an ocean field
as fluid and deep as fathomed blue or green
from its deck I'm capsized by air but anchored
all the same while I swim from Precambrian room
to room listening to the trees washing their leaves
and learning once again how to breathe.

Long Goodbye to Paradise

It happens slowly   the way dawn fills the morning sky
light seeping in   night edging toward the door like the last
guest who stays too long

it happens the way the last handful of leaves
dry as chimes   hang their thin notes in the cooling wind
the wind that will also wrap its hand
across their mouths

and the way rain comes   gathering first in darkening
rooms of cloud before it jumps   its falling a long goodbye
to paradise

it's the way you see someone   sitting and talking   eyes
fixed in the distance which is really their own mind
that small flame like a tongue   their thoughts quick as licks
dissolving when they say   *where was I?*

it happens slowly that you recognize the breath of things
and their drowning   that you hear the little gap in the heartbeat
expanding like a universe   spreading its silence
opening.

Because Everything Is Water

Because I came
from between the beats
in the river of my mother
from the sound of the ocean opening
and closing its door
from the large black room
that is the earwig's solitude
because I came from the space
in the spider's vigil   the place
between ebb and flow

because everything is water
and empty space
nameless and void
I call to it   *Singing Emptiness*
Heart of my Heart   Little Bud
pushing your green fist through your sleeve

I call to it   *Blue Star   Zeta Ophiuchi trailing your scarves*
of cyan fires and rust through the universe
Singing Bowl   your breath defines
my silence
your heart of dust and vapour beating
like rain against this Milky Way   against this small white house.

The Night Is a Boat

The sky is black as a page
before the stars are written   before their infinite soliloquies
their immense speeches that trail off
when they unlock their houses of blue dust

so it's late and I'm driving
there's a man in an open doorway   the doorway hemorrhaging light
all that's visible is his outline   his silhouette backlit
by a room bright as a bleeding star   the chemistry of time
and space never quite fixed

he stands casually
his dog somewhere in the tall grass
he doesn't see the light falling like rain around him
radical photons bleaching the air   the slow fade of cursive
meteors   he doesn't see
that the doorway is a boat   that he's lucent   floating and anchored
to the dark sea as though to a blank page
to that space within a space both made and not made

he doesn't see that the blackness is the light
that the night is a boat   water whispering like grass
in the breeze
so he turns to step inside
as though he's closing the door   turning off the lights
his arms like oars at his side.

Lorca's Ants

After a dream in which I received a letter from Lorca warning
that *intelligence is often the enemy of poetry because it limits too much*
and it elevates the poet to a sharp-edged throne where he forgets
that ants could eat him or that a great arsenic lobster could fall on his head
I get out of bed and waiting for the kettle to boil   reaching for tea
see small chains moving along the windowsill toward me

Lorca's ants are pouring out of the wood as though it were an elevator
workers brown as briefcases overflowing into the upper world
the support beam now cavernous   emptiness enshrined
a grotto in my kitchen where there is nothing to hold up my house
except these slender ropes of ants   muddy as water   spiralled as
                                                                    galaxies
frail as stars holding up the night.

The Yellow Cat

in memory of Eileen Wilton

The yellow cat who floats
outside your window closed
against such things

enters without opening anything
it's late and moonless
on both sides of the glass

he is from a long line
an alchemical cat yellow as a flame
as the rattle of stars on a black plate

his father was large
and green
a lion satisfied with the sun

you're half awake
the room now lit
your mind a silhouette.

A Place Never Photographed

Black as loudspeakers
the crows rough up the sky
clouds double over
the air turns blue as poetry

a shadow glides over the field
dreaming it is an eagle
or a cloud

it is here my home was made
long before I came to
the blueblack overlap
of sky and serrated crows
flying like knives
pinning world to world
black to white
like the negative
of a place never photographed
the ditch of a crow's heart
as he rises and flies
sawing all the names in two.

Throwing the Bones: Moon Song

Other sun
you rise
rubbled in the dim
like a prediction

indifferent ruin
you do what you are
what you have always been
my nighteyes watch you move
bovine slow across the black field
as I sharpen my incisors
on this bit of bastard bone
thrown here and there
for a telling come true

our hunger has just begun
our days are numbered.

Bat Song

Lucifugal as ashes
           from invisible fires
we fly over the earth at night

  dainty mediums

      little satellites

  echolocating

      your dead

entrusting their messages
           slender as sympathy cards
in our fur-and-leather envelopes

you sleep and in your sleep you slip
           below as though to underscore
something you've forgotten

the night's axe falls
little chips we fly out
in all directions

we pull insects
like nails out of the dark
           letting the evening loose

fluttering over your constellations
made from strands of houses
streets lit like amulets

all your burning nights
your beds alight like ships
                in fog

who will show you the night's worth
                the suckle of shadows   who
will remember you to the darkness   the daughters of Nyx

who will watch over your dead   who
                will be your go-between
now that we are weak

reborn too soon
                jacked by the sun and snow
we hunt in winter

                sliding black as commas
into famine white
                as any bridal chamber

    our noses powdered
                like addicts'
we watch our own ghosts   delirious
                fall like snow

in the morning when you wake
                squinting
you are only half yourself

as you begin to remember
you have forgotten
your dead.

A Separate Kingdom (White-Nose Fungus)

White as a straitjacket and dainty as chain lace
I'm modelled by my hosts like winter lingerie

psychrophilic as little chills
I spread myself thin as dust in the hibernacula

my life   cryptic as a spy's   my realm   a separate kingdom

I rouse my hosts   hijack these little brown bats and we fly out
                                                  into the centre
of winter   blindfolded   disoriented as a compass without a needle
limp as junkies sliding down walls

into the chipped white   .
empty as a plate and cold
as our kingdom come.

Initiation

When I first met death
my blood murmured   *I will be your red dress*
my bones echoed   *we will walk in your body of emptiness*
my flesh said   *I will be a sentence*
in the book you burn

and the other part of me
part forest   part ocean
part mouse   part wolf
the part seeded by dust
of meteors and asteroids
and the carbon whispers
of dying stars

that part rose like a wave   like the forest from seed
                                        in time-lapse
like feathers from a shell with cracked teeth
                                        glistening.

When the Stones Wept

The night is falling asleep beneath a grey sheet
doves rearrange their feathers   turn on their lights

they fly in circles   stirring the dawn like spoons

and land in the trees sounding
the call to prayer

all the faces of stones are wet
as memory crawls out of every living thing.

A Red Singing

From time to time they drift in like snow or so it seems
but I suppose it's like moisture on windows   always there
and only visible in winter
like the fingers of trees no longer gloved by leaves

now they walk up and down   up and down the stairs
echoing like pin lights   filaments arcing
your dreams   the ones that fill with strangers all waving
                                        from such a distance
their arms look like feelers reading the air
as though it were a book of invisible narratives

they never speak the language you'd expect   the dead
speak in sound and scent   in the haptics of sheer presence
the weight of the space their absence has made
in the air thickening   clotting like blood
which sounds like singing   a red singing
in the scent of flowers you cannot name
their perfumes blooming and fading
like the rhythm of a woman brushing
her long hair   the hush and slide.

Autobiography

All my histories make a dream
of this

so that now the memory of stone
the grass in its green dress
the pock of soil sleeping in absences
make a life more real than real is

paperweights

holding
this small life of mine
to the world like a note.

The Fourth Bear

after reading From Sarajevo, with Sorrow; *for Goran Simić*

Your bloodstained poems keep me up at night. Words like refugees
huddled in a language not their own. And beneath them, the third
language which is the hardest to learn, the mother tongue
of the country we all knew once. It is not an official language,
which explains why poetry has fallen here, why poets must learn
to live in two places at once as you have done.
It's the animal between your words moving the blue wound around,
quanta-black staining its mouth, the photon vowel. Perhaps it's a wolf,
or a bear, the one left out of the fairy tale. The fourth bear.
Lairing beneath your words, he sleeps lightly, bruining and dreaming
he is a man in winter bent over pages red and white as blood on snow.

Somnambulant Meadows

The night's pelt settles around my shoulders
as I walk along the road   cars like jewellery parked in their boxes
stars behind the sky's curtain waiting
to go on

in the woods and across the fields an invisible river of breath
like the epic sweep of an ageless bear   its flesh hibernating
rushes across fields   roving and voluptuous
as namelessness in search of a name   that small hostel built
of sticks and vowels
all the little dams we build between worlds

along the road are living rooms   somnambulant meadows
where sleepwatchers tune out for the night
sinking in their greenhouses where blue flickers petal
the windows   climb the drapes and shades
shadow play upon shadow play

this is the way our lives are made   in the mothering darkness
of a field or wood   in the flicker of living rooms   in the dimly lit cities
of anthills   their busy kitchens   dens made of little glints
                                        the sting and bleed
of desire

tonight this river   this breath desires smallness   a matter of flesh
the stucco of a stone's coat   the fine edge of blade-lit grass
                                        the defined line
of a stick across a path like a constellation shaping the sky
Ursula returned to her meadow of fur
a simple beginning and end   a waking.

Salt Lick

Winter again and clouds banked up
against the mineral mind   snow mutes the arrogance of *is*
whisper of a tail feather across the snow
a small gloss in the large margin
calligraphy of silence   a clean sweep

so many living off salt   eating snow and tunnelling
it's harder to listen   harder to hear the muffled *is*-ing
everything bound and gagged   white of the wind
fingering the knots   the drag and drop
the sound of zero whistling the *isn't*.

Field of Language (Silent Film)

Clouds scrape the sky
the season thins like hair
trees drop
their gold earrings
becoming rough crutches
for the unseen

goldenrod is leaving
its body   it pales the way a thing does
when its word is born   cord cut

this house I was born to
I've known before   the height of it

and the vertigo

in countries all over the earth
I've slept on pages in drawers
like boarders in dormitories
changing worlds

worlds beyond reach

the cuneiform of cloud
written and rewritten
the syllabary of a sparrow as it flies
through the dusk above
the river's grey scapular

in my scriptoria
dragonflies nib the air
and cicadas blog small as circuits

tell me then
why am I as necessary
as the sky's blue wound

    O

when night opens
like the suitcase you think you've unpacked
you'll have only words
empty and folded clothes
a bit of smoke in their hems

and stars huddled around their campfires
singing songs of vapour and dust

    O

clouds appear to come and go
through the moon's projector
my silent film fills
the landscape's cinema
which is why the faces of stones
flicker in a silver field
a field of language full of the lives taken
and the ones quietly put in their place
the ones you thought were lost but were mistaken.

All the Hidden Places

The summer fades like a powder burn
air on the move again   leaves learning the colour wheel
the sun making shorter appearances as though
it knows the day by heart   the novelty worn off

no longer summer and the geese still sound
like a traffic jam
the sun slides like a painting out of its frame
what I couldn't see earlier
I can see now

I'm sitting on the stoop
listening to little invertebrates
running like zippers through the earth
listening to the light bleed   this world's gegenschein
echoing the galactic glow
pulse of biophotons in the field and trees
the whisper of birds in skeletal leaves
dialects dusted in regolith   dipped in grey crepe

dusk gathers itself like a thought
earwigs slide out and in brown as stitches
buttressing corners and crevices
sewing the damp to the dark   all the hidden places
together in one evening

an evening both short and long enough
for the unseen to appear
like the memory of the slow burn
of childhood or a bird in a tree at dusk
its notes in the air like small moons
the scent of gunpowder
drifting in the dark.

Before the Before

I remember who I was before the before
when my transparent bones fell like rain
and my clear skeleton walked through clouds like walls
and stroked the green animal before it was named

my silver pins held the spider to her galaxy of silk
held the ditches in place   their dark sheets a black canopy
of larval instars echoing my memory of space
and space

I fastened flesh to the emptiness and held that emptiness
close to the body   that vastness flush with the mind
you know the one   the one that shines
like water beading on a river of fur
like so many breathless eyes.

Where the Unseen Gathers

His eyes were blue   clear as water before it freezes
this was how he was able to see through me

his fur was black and white   equiluminant
so he appeared to be running
blurring into grey like water falling horizontally
matter is spirit moving slowly enough
to be seen
he practiced for invisibility

somewhere out there in the huge subatomic
somewhere in the immense realm of here
beyond the politics of the seen
where the unseen gathers like the heart
of dark matter's gravitational pull
he waits for me to catch up.

A Small Feast

It's late October and the maples stand
leaves like little bags of blood hanging in the air
the measured drip   the little feast

the bead factory of rosehips is closing for the season
a blue rinse of asters gathers for small talk
stones are turning off their lights   calling
the bloodless to breakfast   to this small feast
this light in the vein   arterial glow like sweat
on the road that ran all night in its sleep
all the little kindlings in the earth
now risen   gone viral as morning
when shadows turn the other cheek
before Lazarusing and the stones stand open
as mouths.

A Word No One Knows

Neither subject nor object
I come from the static

at the edge of burdock
from the silence in the centre of its battle mace

I'm the bloom
of horror in the heart's dissolve

the yellow petals of carbon
stroking the dying star

I'm the little thorn
the pebble in your mind's shoe

the hollow in the feather's shaft
the overlap of *this* and *that*

I'm the hyphen
marrying *I* to *Thou*

a dash or ellipsis
from over the border

of speech
the land discarded

by this human country
I'm made daily

of gesture and intent
insistent as the shine

lit beneath the flesh.

Mysterium Tremendum

I remember my mother and father
when they were whole
when I was motherless
fatherless and orphan
of none
when stillness and silence
reigned at the core
where *all* and *not*
were at once
there and not there

and emptiness bloomed
an eye in the dark
Terrible Immense
Beautiful One.

Last Rites

A hawk embering on a branch
razors folded tight against his body

he opens like a switchblade
a spark flying into the autumn field

his wings beating out the fire of himself
he leaves a trail of smoke in the air

some ashes on the earth.

Songs of the Afterlife

The grass is changing its brown dress
the tips of trees are opening their eyes
like periscopes

I prefer the slow motion of things
living and dying in real time
not the time-lapse of the mind

nests are going up like barns
the worm hunters have returned   pulling
elastics from the earth's hair

cars drive faster
their windows rolled down
like sleeves
invisible fists of music
punch the air

another long winter dead
and buried
the thaw and slide
of days into spring
the cut and paste
the death of death brings

nights blooming with songs
of the afterlife
amphibious urge rolling out
its green carpet
the stars like paparazzi
amongst all the dark flowers.

Yellow Birds in Cages of Water

This afternoon the poplars are carrying
their baskets up from the river
each one a lantern
of yellow birds in a cage of sticks
silver sticks the colour of water late
for a fire
in the field below them
dandelions in their grey afros
sway like a gospel choir
a sharp-shinned hawk is poised
for an air strike
this afternoon the grass is casting
its shadows thin as knives   black as slivers
into the earth's palm   styptic nowhere in sight
only the sound of wings blond as oars
rippling the field
only the light from little fires
yellow birds in their cages of water   rowing.

Reading

The line is a stick
and a branch
layered with other sticks
on a bed of paper

the updraft
a thin whistle
almost audible

so that the reader's head
is cocked like a dog's

and when she looks up
from the page
her house is on fire.

Tree of Sorrows

It could be the sky
or it could be water
it could be the grass
in November's wind
dry as bells along the road
or the hunchbacked anthills
breaking through the snow

or a scold of crows
a bit of roadkill in their guts
eyes bright with drink
the world too fluid

it could be a man driving
through a city
a child beside him
black patent shoes on her feet
her body braced
for the accident
that is their life

that child grown
a stick of charcoal in her hand
the man dreaming of walking again
among the living

it could be
that the dreams of the dead
return to the world
as bells beside a road
as a sketch of crows on Judgement Day
one crow for each sorrow
shining like a patent leather shoe
in a tree in winter.

When Night

The moon is stuck in the trees
a ball abandoned
by children dead and gone
dawn is lifting the night like weights
it stretches   rises from its bed

birds fly back to their bodies
colours emerge from their hiding places

shadows fade
as all countries do   leaders overthrown
borders redrawn

soon the trees will be boarded up
for the season   the moon will pull
a black sheet over its face
and come back from the dead
the way so many do
when *night is not night enough*
to remember them   mouths open as roses
their voices waxing   curved as petals
blackening time   falling through space
death loves us
it loves us not.

A House Waiting to Be Haunted

White mallows appear in a corner of the field
like nurses conferring in a ward
where all the patients succumb one by one
alone with the alone

in this way the field grows round
as a sigh   a whisper come home
vowels left out   a house of elisions
where the dead are written but not pronounced.

A Floating Forest

Autumn overwritten by November *dreich*
skysmoke and smoulder blotting out the sun
the earth off-grid and flowing in cursive
like a river writing and rewriting its name

shiver of feathers   I ripple air
a barred owl   in my dialect of silence
my body of knives and ashes a floating forest
face an empty plate   my eyes   morgue doors
painted on black water
watching from just that distance
anthropomorphizing the human

everywhere I look a hotspot
candling the heart of a vole   the marrow of a hare
a mouse running like a fuse to the river
everywhere I turn I hear the small rush.

Soliloquy of a Field Mouse

What moves the reddened wood
of my blood
the brightened eye of my eye its wick
lit by a river trembling with fire

what novas in the forest
immaterial pulse of feathers
grey as waves
against a shore I cannot name

what was I once that I should be again
what precedes me will remain
when I'm dissolved into the ethereal speech of grass
gone green again

I will leave my body as I have done before
a small meal for my predators and my kind
on this field's floor

I will spread unseen like water spilling
from a glass
the current that moves between
sibling things

what pervades me
for a taste of the contained
the defined world both elegant
and maimed

what sustains the forms
that haunt the particular life
what claw
what claw of water
hunts me down.

Flying the Words Home

After weeks of wordlessness I hear a cry
this second language   spawn of silence

through the window I see an eagle
its black apron and white hood brooding
over a field   Fair Executioner
Maker of the twitch and tremble
the consonant brown of a rabbit

and the crash
that has only one
survivor
its black bag of a heartbeat
flying the words home.

After Winter

After winter the cornfields
are rows of burnt matchsticks

skeletal stalks and blackened earth

not one of us remembers the fire
only a long dream full of cold white smoke.

A White Room Full of White Birds

August and clouds are backcombing
over the bald blue
hummingbirds en garde and hovering
like green *x*'s crossing the days out
more good weather behind than ahead
there is less I understand than I once did

names relinquish nothing

so I watch clouds shadow-knitting
throwing their black voices on the bay
(what is the sea but the memory of land)
never the same cloud twice   never the same ground
as the bay waves its white flag
and drowns   an iceberg   prodigal glacier
rearranging itself in a larger and larger room
melting its way home
which is the glacier
which the cloud

☽

afternoon shadows recline
tired effigies   black *gisants* for the turn and tilt
goldenrod deepening
a little every day
knowing only its comings and goings
but not its name
so it bows

to the hunger of finches
inflorescence of yellow on gold
which is the flower
and which the bird

◯

more clouds moving in
the sky now a blur   no figure no ground
just a white room full of white birds
not a cage in sight.

Spring Equinox

The earth is slowly peeling its white gloves off
you can see them lying in the woods
as though dropped by winter's dog
as he follows his master across the sky
fingers of earth showing through
pointing.

The Last Silence

Are you still there   my friend
are your ears still saluting
the silence

do you still bury what you cannot bear
to lose   as we all do   as we all do
all the bones you planted
never grew   it is the same for all of us

are your eyes still filled with the blue
water   sky   the glacier's crevasse

are you there when I sometimes hear you
an echo across the years
the click of your nails on the floor
like an abacus
solving the last silence

my friend   are you still sitting
in the darkness   alert at the threshold
the one we never know is there
until we've crossed it.

The Earth's Thaumaturgy

The sun is climbing its blue mountain
birds open their curtains   fly like shards into the glass

the green office opens   woodpeckers type on brown keyboards
squirrels file and misfile items of great importance

like me the flowers open their blue eyes

crows work mad as surgeons
on the night's carnage

pulling a single black thread through the day

◯

the city is sleepwalking again
hands parked like cars in the sleeves of streets

it dreams it is outside its body
sliding out of apartment   lot and subdivision   grid and graph

it dreams it is outside itself   outside of culture
which is *what's left after you've forgotten everything*

it wanders outside its skin thin as civilization
the further it walks the more it's tranced into flight

by the darkness where it can see the stars   time come and time gone
where it is a wood   a valley   a river unalienated by pettiness
                                                    by vanity

where it can again expand like a universe
or breathe like a wolf   running novas

you   darkness   that I come from
I love you more than all the fires

that fence in the world

     ○

below   you are sleeping
curled around a dog

I can't tell the fact of it
that is not in my nature

I only know
you are sleeping

that *we sleep in language*
if language does not come to wake us with its strangeness

and that there is a dog in your arms
like a blue-eyed wolf and any star there ever was

trailing the end of a thread black as a crow

     ○

the silence is childrening
like the shadows of clouds on snow

you are dreaming you are a city
you are dreaming you are light

your hands in your pockets
your dogs in the sky

the black knot of a crow tightens
against the day's wound

the earth   old thaumaturge   turns
the sun climbs its blue mountain

and lets the dogs go   making the night young again.

As the Crow Flies

A crow defrags the sky
impasto of clouds above the shorthand of insects
voicethread of poplars fills the air
as the *terra nullius* of stones   *the fallen eyes of angels*
read the Akashic field where every wingbeat is outlined
and impressed   every cricket's mantra grafted
every voicethread quivers and carries as though over water
across a riverbed of stones   their breath silver as flares
breaking the surface like memory's air kiss   the trace
of a small black *x*   flying.

The Animate Breath

It's early spring or late winter   depending
and the river is shedding its skin
piling its icy scales along the banks
as it slides like a tongue through the earth panting
its animate breath   the slow melt
of appearances into the shine

I'm walking along its banks
near the end of my fiftieth winter
though winter is numberless as the gap
between the living and the dead
the white syntax in the earth's text

above me   murmuration of light poised to dissolve
like hundreds of starlings into one mind
geese haven't yet returned to herd the sky
so it hangs   pale as a Monet
over what passes for a large room
a room all-encompassing and round
as this suburban earth
a planet both too immense and too small
for our paradoxes

in the woods long-horned beetles are rearranging
the landscape   laying spruce down
one on top of the other   making their own pyres
as we all do eventually
ellipses of sparrows dot the sky
hoofmarks in the cloven snow trail off

an accident of pheasant tracks   ideograms
pointing in all directions

clouds soft as erasers rub the light out
as the afternoon passes without moving
the way deer evaporate in their vespered fur
near the river   only their breath still visible
as clouds fallen to earth in their white saris.

A Broken Necklace

Winter's breath has come to the end of its sentence
now cutlery floats up through the soil   green tines
push into the air and cups appear like flowers

the grass unpacks   stones scattering pale as beads
from a broken necklace   the necklace the dead once wore
to keep them in the underworld

○

they move from one unknown place to another
from darkness to darkness   from flame to flame
moth-eaten as shadows flying over a field fallen with names

○

one rests beneath floral sheets
all her jewellery   some rings and a strand of pearls
removed so she can float around the room

her river of hair is matted as grass beneath snow
her voice escapes like blood from a bandage
splattering the room with ruby vowels   animal sounds

○

another rests his handless hand on your shoulder
and another is the sound of a blue dog
pushing a bowl around the floor
lapping emptiness like water

○

a door opens
voices carry as though over water
so that the field melts into a banquet hall in spring
and laughter scatters like glass flowers

○

O Wordless Invisible Synapse
Little Sting and Stirrer of Bloodlight
be with us now
and at the hour of our death

○

and you   most dear   already you know
my voice like the moon's
through her shawl of clouds

this is how I learned to love the dead
their lives unstrung
like stones in a field in early spring.

On the Cusp of Spring

It's been years now since you drifted
into the silence   years since you dug
a bed in the snow for us
since we lay down   your tail over your nose
your forepaw over my shoulder
the blue of your eyes unreal   unreal
and the stars
played their tricks with time

years it's been
or perhaps we've not met yet
not eyed one another warily
nor made our constellation of two
Canis Minor
not yet risen   not yet
perhaps we haven't parted
those last days still to come

on the cusp of spring
snow becomes water once again
running

perhaps that is why I think of you
the way you ran   blue-eyed
as water when I was winter.

Where Once There Were Stairs

February   pale month   rider moon   the dead gather
like trees in their white coats   hushed as doctors

except for the girl splashed in red on a black horse gusting
across a snowy field like a glass rose blown
by February's thorny wind

I don't know if the dead cling to us
or we to them

the rose blows into spring
the wind dies down

a cat grey as the sky leaps through
the wall where once there were stairs
chasing a mouse all the way to paradise.

Still the Blue

I still have what you gave me
all those years ago   the blue
set in the centre of a glacier
the river wrapped in red   salmon tying
and untying themselves to the water
the silence
in which you sat for hours outside the door
the silence
you brought in
the silence you shook when it was wet
and laid down when it was tired   you next to it
throwing your forepaw over its shoulder

I still have the silence old friend
still the blue
to this day my head bows
when I near the river
all those red ribbons opening
and you just beneath the surface.

A Name I Once Wore

I'm walking where air shivers into wind
and the wind folds like the tip of a page
marking my place on a new trail

freezing rain tinsels the air   turns to snow treading water
falling like static   the white noise of January

the spectral chair of a tree
creaks with the weight of memory
a weight that spreads along its thin arms
like the fire they once carried into the forest
wolf chorus just behind the bright curtain

the landscape turns back like a page
read too quickly
italics of trees legible against the grey sky
like a name I once wore
written as though on a door opening
to rooms without walls
where I wait in one form or another
for those who preceded me here

to this place scented
by a little whiff
of the infinite
snow falling in January
a martyr of wet dogs
drying by the fire.

Book of Obscure Sorrows

A backwashed sky   the sound of a river in the birch leaves
like water having an out-of-body experience
before it freezes

goldenrod   mullein   burdock   all in the brown study
this shoulder season in which I walk
where the only wildflowers left have dust in their eyes

a pair of bald eagles preside over the field like judges
death sentences hang in the air   winter's debridement
not far off

in Elsie's field   hay bales scarecrow the cold to come
sunflowers stand like microphones without singers
nodal lines becoming visible
as the breeze rocks the field to sleep beneath the memory
of hawking dragonflies   green darners fluorescent as mobiles

grasshoppers have left their exoskeletons behind
pinches of chitin   little armatures abandoned
after the unveiling
there's a nest of mice incubating in the grass
their last breaths seeding the air

deer graze and look up   graze and look up
from the book of obscure sorrows   from this field
bedding down for the season   the breeze slowly
turning its pages like a reader no longer there.

Substance to Ether

My blood has faded
from being outside my flesh

my bones have thinned to a wish
for visibility

my face is the face you've forgotten
eroded as a stone by the worry of elements

I'm blank as a screen
for all your earthly needs

from substance to ether
I've all but disappeared

you say you can see me
but you cannot

you see the moon remembering
the sun.

A Room No Longer There

Tonight there's not much to say
so I will just mention
that it's not yet
winter and the poplars
have taken their vow of silence
that the moon is blacklisted
and holed up elsewhere

that the locust tree
stands like a woman
who's dropped her brown gloves
that a squirrel has misplaced something
in the leaves
and the deer are empty as rooms
where the weight of frostbitten fruit
hangs in the air like myth

in the distance
rain is opening its umbrella
and soon the river will slur
its words

I will just mention
that it's so dark the shadows
have all stayed home
their children under curfew
turning in for the night
like knives washed and dried

the glint of their blade-tips
a few stars spinning
in a room no longer there.

Lumen Naturae

In this forest of skin   bark and earth
molecular chaperones are signalling
flames wet as burning water
this is the flicker of stars sitting up
in their caskets   open as shadows
lucid as the wound closest to the sun's
black suns I can't quite
reach so I lean in   lean in
and it's as if the whole world is an ember
cradled in the elements
and I'm listening or praying or writing a poem
which are all the same thing and remembering
something both mine and not my own at all
like an unfed wick bending to pick
up the fire from another smouldering thing
bowing to untie the thin ropes of smoke
from the earth

this is how I know the world is burning
this is how I hear the earth's haglight
cackling.

Ode with an Elegy around Its Edges

The sky is a bruised falling this January evening
nightblood on the rise   a black tide coming in
as I sit watching the fire   flames rubbing their hands
for warmth   for what they can't hold   rivers of light
slipping through their fingers

I've cherished the *isn't*-ness of the world   broken
heartedness eking out its living   showing me the possible
I've sung my lullabies to orphans of the earth
and to the orphanage itself   dismembered
by our own absence   our day's amnesia

because I know no other way
every elegy has an ode at its centre
every ode has an elegy around its edges

○

embedded as stars in the invisible
we are the blind beheld   short-lived as sparks
just before they catch and spread the dark rumour
eternal gossips

so my life has been a practice of sitting up
with the night as though with a neglected child
of listening to its blurry desire   its voice of smoke
everything it isn't gathering into an immense
presence   I've listened to its shunnedness
its banishments   its tongue stumbling over

its own blackened name
and how it is tired of being so large
as alone as a great bear without a body of its own
the one our small world turns and turns within
how we turn away
from its shapelessness   how we desire
clear   bright   constellated names

☽

night never falls but rises
a black cup to our lips
from which we'd rather not drink
but drink we do eventually   ready or not
olly olly oxen free   as the seeds we are
open to the depths
yellow floatinghearts in the nightsky
petals small as flames   holding
hands beneath the water.

As the Day Keeps

Autumn arrives a bit out of breath
leaves clear the rattle from their throats
the wind picks up
the day moving it a little to the left
to the right and back again
rain unpacks itself all over the landscape

you are away
so I practice loss
in the same way as the day
keeps its hours and loses some light
in the same way as the rain
falling from the sky's breath
reincarnates itself

the petunias we planted
fade like bruises
goldenrod ghosts the field
Septembering

the hummingbirds have flown on
leaving their shadows behind
so many small black dresses
one for each day they loved.

After Midnight

There is a speech made of silence.
An obstacle may be a path.
—Shachar Mario Mordechai (translated by Lisa Katz)

Clouds written west to east
moon rising round as a dial
turning the volume down
on the day's epilogue

it's after midnight
when all our words are in the morgue
and a language without a name
remembers us

its light is deafening
so aspens tremble like mice
as an owl pellet drops
and fireflies blitz the field
going off like distant gunfire
we can't hear

it's after midnight
when shadows grow   watered by moonlight
their roots illuminated manuscripts
written only on the verso   beneath the cadence of grass
where all the worlds come together

and apart again
like the phases of the moon
which tonight is gravid as a spider

climbing her web of trees
to wrap another word   shroud it
in her silk until it rises again.

Siamese Forests

Late in the year's day and the sky sags
light turns its back to the world   focuses on inner things
fading in   fading out
like a thought barely caught or the memory of summer's riot
flowers bleeding out and weeds protesting
our sense of order   our small war with burdock

I'm surrounded by the earth's introversion   the sky slowly drained
grass returning to its deeper self   flowers leaving their bodies
to science   deer ticks walking on their grass stilts   blood bulbs
waiting for their last bloom
in the orchard the earth is churned
by Dionysian deer   paradise consumed   a bit of Eden in the entrails

late afternoon   autumn in camouflage
as I walk across leaves the colour of small fires
like burial rafts on the ground's sea
I remember the prescience of spring   buds and shoots
the birth of grief in all things born
I walk chaperoned
by trees joined at the root   Siamese forest beneath my feet

○

above me   a hawk sits in his body's darkroom
waiting for a mouse to develop
dusk metastasizes   blurring the particular
figure and ground dissolving   adjusting my view
it's a quiet death   an ordinary passing as the day excarnates

here in the forest's hospice where I rest below eons
in the form of a great spruce   *axis mundi*
and know this is the tree I would rest against in death
as some peoples did long ago   so that the tree in growth
embraces the dead one's bones.

Feeding the Dead

I leave these words out
for the dead   for their webbed whispers   their filigree need
so they may not hunger

for trees in their green cellophane in spring
for the egg-white shine of starlings
lacquering the sky

I leave these words
so that they may not hunger any longer
after cell or bone or heart   the regret of flesh not fleshed out

that they may feel
the mouth of their invisibility close around these words
like dusk savouring the day   the taste of a memory unmade.

Shadow Play

The sky described
is not the sky

the stone that's named
is not the stone that is

just ask it
it will confirm
its preverbal reality

words are brutes
beating their elders

which is why the stone is face down
its back calloused

and the sky keeps its distance

all language is shadow play
a puppet show   Punch and Judy
battaccio in hand

it's a matter of degree
like *rain* or *snow*
and all the names between

standing in for water
in all
its falling dreams.

Transmigration

It's February   when the dead rise
like water and fall like snow   raining backwards
their voices tearing like paper
cracking like branches   those orphans of trees
blowing across the bare road   a little rattle here
a spark there like a stressed syllable   a little fire in its hair.

Afterfeathers

Decades ago I had wanted to marry
God and now I think I did even though
I no longer believe and don't know what *God* means
the adagio of a spider's legs   the wingbrushed sky
polished as a forehead   clouds remembering a house
of water and its small rooms of rain
our desire for wholeness that now seems a nostalgia
a form of ouroboric incest or perhaps
numen mentis   bidden memory of dustlight
shine and scribble of the illegible

○

I believe in chemicals awash in the sea
hydrogen and oxygen   sodium
nitrogen and especially carbon   *genius loci*
of light   patron saint of space
I believe in the light pollution of denial
I believe in solar power
and the sun's nova to come
and in all the particles   dark energies and matter
I can't see   I believe we're outnumbered

I believe in the moon
and her maria darkened by iron
the extrasolar systems   the oldest star found
over eleven billion light years old
with its handful of exoplanets
one for each finger pointing

to all the matryoshka universes
I believe in ignorance   especially my own

I believe in the salty bark of the locust tree
that feeds some animals in winter
and that the death of that tree is meaning
that the photons of the chickadee's eye
have travelled longer than I can imagine
that the unborn   chanting like an old nun in her sleep
that the snort of a deer   are burning worlds
and the cloven marks I see everywhere
are hinges opening and closing
a dusk the colour of a dove's feather   a crow's quill
as he darkens the story
marrying the told to the untold
the corporeal to the incorporeal   little weights in the air
little spaces in the earth   weights and spaces small enough
for a god or two and their auguries of the *here* and the *not here*
I believe in the barbs locking *what is* to *what isn't*
in all the afterfeathers keeping us warm.

NOTES

Because Everything Is Water
Zeta Ophiuchi is a runaway star plowing through space dust.

Lorca's Ants
The italicized lines are from Frederico Garcia Lorca.

Throwing the Bones
Throwing the bones is a method of divination.

All the Hidden Places
Gegenschein is the counterglow of sun's light scattered by interplanetary dust.

A biophoton is a photon of non-thermal origin in the visible and ultra-violet spectrum emitted from a biological system.

Regolith is the layer of unconsolidated rocky material covering bedrock and is found on earth, the moon, Mars, and some asteroids; according to astronauts, lunar regolith/dust/soil has the scent of gunpowder.

Where the Unseen Gathers
The italicized lines are from Pierre Teilhard de Chardin.

When Night
The first italicized phrase is borrowed from Franz Kafka: "That is why one can never be alone enough when one writes, why there can never be enough silence around one when one writes, why even night is not night enough."

A Floating Forest
Dreich is a Scottish word for grey, cold, damp, and miserable.

The Earth's Thaumaturgy
The first italicized line is borrowed from Jules Renard: "Culture which is what's left after you have forgotten everything."

The second italicized passage is from Rainer Maria Rilke: "You, darkness, that I come from / I love you more than all the fires / that fence in the world."

The third italicized passage is from Robert Kelly: "We sleep in language if language does not come to wake us up with its strangeness."

As the Crow Flies
Defragging is the process of consolidating fragmented data on a volume (such as a hard disk or a storage device).

The phrase "the fallen eyes of angels" is from Gwendolyn MacEwen.

Akasha is from Sanskrit and Vedic meaning "space"; Akashic Field theory hypothesizes a field of information as the substance of the cosmos; the fundamental energy and information-carrying field that informs not just the current universe, but all universes past and present.

Lumen Naturae
Paracelsus incorporated the Gnostic notion of nature's light into his own thinking on the light in nature which he saw, paradoxically, as both temporal and eternal. C. G. Jung's studies of alchemy and Paracelsus in particular led him to write: "This light is the *lumen naturae* which illuminates consciousness, and the *scintillae* are germinal luminosities shining forth from the darkness of the unconscious" and "...*lumen naturae* is the light of the darkness itself" (C. G. Jung, *Collected Works,* vol 8 and 13 respectively).

"Lucidity is the wound closest to the sun" is a line from René Char.

"How can there be laughter, how can there be pleasure, when the whole world is burning?" is from *The Dhammapada*.

Ode with an Elegy around Its Edges

Yellow floatingheart is a water-lily-like plant with small yellow blossoms that grows in lakes and rivers.

Shadow Play

The opening lines of this poem echo a passage from the *Tao Te Ching*, by Lao Tzu (as translated by Arthur Waley).

Afterfeathers

Ouroboric incest is described by Erich Neumann in *The Origins and History of Consciousness*, Volume I as a return to the Great Mother/World Parents, a desire by the developing ego for complete surrender/union/reunion and dissolution/death.

Afterfeathers are the downy, lower barbs at the base of the feather shaft.

ACKNOWLEDGEMENTS

Some of these poems have appeared in *Contemporary Verse 2, Eighteen Bridges, Prairie Fire, Atlanta Review* (US), *Written River* (US), and *Reliquiae* (UK), as well as in the anthologies *Poems from Planet Earth* (Leaf Press) and *Poet to Poet* (Guernica Editions) and in the Contemporary Poetry Series by Corbel Stone Press (UK). I'm grateful to the editors for their support and interest.

I'm grateful to Arts Nova Scotia for financial support.

Thanks to Don and Mary for two decades of deep friendship.

Thank you to Wayne Boucher for his gracious permission to use his painting for the cover.

Thank you to everyone at Brick.

O

For Graham.
In memory of Mary McCarthy and those who've gone ahead.

JULIA MCCARTHY is originally from Toronto, Canada. She spent a decade living in the US, most notably in Alaska and Georgia. She also lived in Norway and spent significant time in South Africa before returning to Canada and settling in rural Nova Scotia where she has worked as a potter to support her poetry habit. She is the author of two previous poetry collections: *Stormthrower* (Wolsak & Wynn, 2002) and *Return from Erebus* (Brick Books, 2010), the latter of which received the Canadian Authors Association Poetry Award.